SEO Standards for Beginners

This book is dedicated to all the individuals and business owners interested in learning more about what SEO really is, why they need to employ SEO tactics in their online marketing campaign and who want to know the basics so that they can avoid the scammers who won't do anything more than take their money and confuse them with as much jargon talk as possible.

SEO Standards for Beginners

What is SEO?

SEO is an acronym in the Internet tech world that stands for "Search Engine Optimization."

There is a great deal of talk and hype out in viral cyberspace about what SEO and different ideas about what works and what doesn't. This can be extremely confusing to the people truly interested in learning about SEO because research on this topic generates a great deal of contradictory information.

Do not be deceived, this contradictory information is placed out for the public to grab for two specific reasons.

1. If people are confused or mislead, they will more easily fail in their SEO attempts, creating an advantage for the SEO professionals in being able to beat out the competition for organic search engine result pages.

2. Many "SEO Professionals" do not know what they are talking about. There is no formal education for SEO and no way to block those who have no clue about the industry from starting their own "SEO Company" and raking in the bucks from the unsuspecting business owners.

So then again, you may be asking…. "What is SEO or Search Engine Optimization?"

SEO is the process through which a business website is optimized in order to begin showing up more prominently in the search engine result pages.

Ultimately, people want the most exposure for their business, as it is highly believed and proven that through exposure, increased sales are possible. If they can't find you….they can't buy from you!

One thing that is not commonly understood, however, is that it takes much more than merely receiving exposure to actual "close the deal" on sales. Unfortunately, many business owners get the idea that if the public could just see that they are offering a service or product, which the public would choose to buy from them.

This is not the case.

However, it is true that you must first receive the exposure in order to take the rest of the actions necessary in reaching your bottom-line.

This is where SEO comes into place.

SEO may also help you when your SEO service is also providing you with call to action content that encourages the readers to call you and to purchase from you, but this is an additional piece of the puzzle and not what most people are thinking about when they think search engine optimization.

Consider now the number of websites that are actually online. If you have at all followed the progress of the Internet marketplace, you will likely be aware of the fact that new websites are being built and published online at alarming speed and that this means that your competition online is likely increasing on a daily basis.

SEO should be the process by which you fight the battle against the websites of other companies that are older than you and that are springing up from day to day.

The methods employed in your website development will have to make a bold statement to the search engine companies that your business provides the best source of information regarding the particular product or service you offer and that people who are directed to view your website will not be disappointed.

But how can you let the search engine companies know that you are going to answer the call of their customers with exceptional proficiency?

You guessed it….SEO….

NOT A SIMPLE TASK

SEO is not one or two actions that you or your web team can complete to let the search engine companies know you are credible, legitimate and ready to inform their audience and yours via your website.

It is a complex and task-heavy project that must encapsulate a large variety of efforts and actions in order to be successful.

Not only is there a great deal of work where a large number of details must be considered in order to meet SEO standards, but the search engine companies like to change the rules on occasion, providing the lovely sense of frustration for business owners who want to just do what they are supposed to do and then leave it at that to be found online.

Additionally, an individual without any web coding knowledge whatsoever is up for a daunting experience due to the fact that a large amount of search engine optimization education and work requires knowledge and understanding of HTML.

.

SEO Resources

There is a bright side to counter the complexity of SEO however. This bright side lies in the fact that search engine companies do provide a measure of assistance in meeting with their web standards for search engine optimization.

At this point in time, Google is the most active search engine, holding more than 65% of the search engine traffic and there is very little indication that they will let up in their fight to remain number one in their industry.

As such, it is extremely important to learn that Google continuously provides information and updates to assist people who want to have their websites optimized and showing up in the search engine listings at high results page levels.

In fact, there are so many resources that Google provides, that it can sometimes be easy to get lost in the mass of it all.

One place that is very good to look in order to get your SEO information directly from the source ..... specifically from the company that you are attempting to please....is Google Webmaster Tools.

You can find Google Webmaster Tools by getting on your computer and putting this URL in the address bar: http://www.google.com/webmasters/

Depending on what you are trying to accomplish, you may or may not have to either have or create a Google account in order to gain full access to the resources available through Google Webmaster Tools.

Another bright spot in the effort to find good, reliable information that is not provided by some SEO hack only interested in seeing you fail…. Is to realize that Google even puts out videos on YouTube, where you can watch and learn many important details regarding basic and advanced SEO standards that many SEO professionals, who are not doing their homework, do not even know.

Google also has a blog that is rich in content and information and surprisingly has a very small following, considering the following of pop culture blogs and even other, non-direct tech blogs that more people seem to get their information from, rather than going directly to the source.

If you really feel like doing some intensive, but excellently productive reading, then you should visit this link: http://static.googleusercontent.com/external_content/untrusted_dlcp/www.google.com/en/us/webmasters/docs/search-engine-optimization-starter-guide.pdf to read through Google's Search Engine Optimization Starter Guide.

Why Didn't I Know I Could Learn SEO from Google?

Interesting question, no?

Again, we go back to the beginning two reasons that there is a great deal of contradictory information posted online about what SEO is and about various successful SEO practices.

Too many search engine optimization companies are terrified that if you could learn even part of what they know, that you might just want to do the work for yourself and stop paying them!

This may be a valid fear in some respects, but it is also an unfortunate misunderstanding about the nature of business and technology.

Here's the fact. If everyone wanted to be a billionaire like Bill Gates or even just spend hours upon hours in front of their computer screens like computer geeks do, then the world would be a completely technologically proficient and independently running society, where even IT support desks were never required.

If someone is not interested in spending time in front of a computer, they are going to hire someone else to spend time in front of a computer for them.

If companies were aware of the amount of work that must go into successful SEO, then they would better realize and be appreciative of the ability to pay a 3rd party SEO service, rather than hiring 1 – 10 employees of their own to do the work and having to continuously train them and stay on top of them to make sure that they are remaining alert regarding all of the latest Internet technology developments.

Companies who are more informed regarding SEO are going to be less unreasonable and increasingly willing to pay for the valuable service that a true SEO professional will provide.

They will be less likely to fire their SEO service when they are not on page 1 of Google in the first few weeks and may even be more likely to notice the increased call volume they are receiving as a result of their search engine optimization company's efforts.

Unfortunately, getting this through the heads of SEO Companies is not always easy or possible and as a result, we continue to find a great deal of misleading information online and a lack of direction for the common business owner to easily realize that they can simply go to Google's many available and free resources for learning more about search engine optimization and tips on implementing successful SEO strategies.

SEO Basics

To better understand how SEO works, it is important to take a moment to think about how people use search engines.

Today, phone books are becoming increasingly obsolete, as more and more people are realizing how easily they can type what they want to find into the search engine and instantly receive results on where to go and what they want to find.

Websites are also more entertaining than phone book pages and this is an additional draw for Internet users.

Why spend time searching for the phone book in the house and then dirtying your fingers on newspaper-type print as you turn page after page to locate a business location that you hope is good and that is near you, when you can simply type what you want into a search engine and not only find a long list of business choices, but also can see reviews on those businesses to see what other customers thought about the company or location that you are thinking about visiting or buying from?

It makes absolutely no practical sense to use a standard telephone book any longer and the only people who still do use these are the technologically impaired, those without sufficient Internet speed and access, or people who are simply old-fashioned and long for the days past when advanced technology meant a better cushion on the saddle for the horse ride to town.

There's nothing wrong with preferring the old days and the old ways. It just isn't practical in a fast-paced world or while living a hectic lifestyle. Maybe the answer is that we all just need to slow down, but here in reality, that's not happening any time soon and people will continue to take advantage of the ability to do more in a much shorter amount of time.

Whether you call it laziness or increased productivity opportunities, it's all the same result. The Internet rules the show.

How Do People Find Things in Search Engines?

To find what you want online, you have to visit a search engine or business directory. Once you reach this hotspot in cyberspace, you then need to communicate to the search engine what it is you want to find.

How do you do this?

It's simple! Type the words that you think of into the search engine query field and hit "enter."

Those words that you use have a special significance and are called "Key Phrases."

Key phrases are the SEO element that you must better understand in order to begin comprehending anything SEO related.

When you type what you want to find or learn more about into a search engine query box, the search engine company uses those words with a scan or "spidering" of all the websites that seem to match the category that that key phrase would fit into.

But how do they know what websites are about which topic?

Simple again…They have to ask themselves….or rather, their search engine algorithms have to determine, what words in what website pages match or are related to the key phrase words that you typed into their question box.

For example, if you were to ask me a question about horse shoes, I would have to think for a moment about every reference to horse shoes that I ever thought about, read about or heard about.

It is only from that recollection that I could give you an answer on the spot.

If I had a bunch of reference books in front of me and wanted to give you an answer based out of those reference books, I would look for the book that I either knew already talked about horse shoes, or I would look for the book that had some sort of related word in the title or related picture on the cover.

Bear in mind now, however, that search engine

spiders cannot read words out of pictures the way

that the human brain can come up with words

based on images.

What the computer programs can do though is look at the coding that was used to post those pictures and see if any of the words in the coding used to create the page with the pictures had any reference to horse shoes.

Also important to recognize though is that if you ask the computer search engine to tell you about horse shoes and it has 5,000 "books" or websites to choose from, some of which have pictures only with brief descriptions of horse shoes connected to the images, while others have pages and pages of web content describing horse shoes, you are more likely to receive the results that are more information heavy, unless of course, you typed in "horse shoe pictures."

Another way the search engine is going to determine whether or not they are providing you with a good result to your question is based on popularity.

Popularity does not mean, as was previously thought in the golden years of Internet technology, the most commonly visited website, because the fact that a website is visited regularly does not mean it is a great resource for the specific topic you are interested in.

However, if a large number of other people or websites have made a point to remark that a specific website is a great resource for horse shoes….perhaps by linking to that website in connection with a horse shoe discussion, then that website has received popularity votes that are actually on topic and make the search engine companies think that their customers will be happy if they also refer them to this website as an answer to the "horse shoes" question.

This particular method of determining which website to display at the top of search engine results pages is connected to the phrase back-linking and link building that you may already have heard about if this is not your first exposure to the world of search engine optimization.

However, before you can get anyone to legitimately link back to your website as being a great place to find information on a specific topic, you have to get your website to provide that great information on the topic and let the search engine companies know too that you are providing a resource for that topic, or that match up with those key phrases, by including both the key phrases, synonyms of the key phrases and actually informative content regarding those key phrases in the writing and code of your website.

If you sell horse shoes, but your website never mentions that phrase, then you are making it difficult for the search engines to know that they should display your web pages for horse shoe results and in turn, you are preventing your website from showing up in the search engine results where horse shoe enthusiasts would be able to find you and then link back to you as being a great place to learn more about horse shoes or to buy horse shoes from.

This book, SEO Standards for Beginners, has been written to encourage you to take some time to analyze your SEO methods and whether or not you are taking the most basic of actions regarding your websites by paying attention to the most basic of all SEO elements, the key phrases that you want to show up as a result for when Internet users and your potential customers type what they are looking for into the search engine query field.

What you have read thus far should inspire you to think about ways that you can better connect readers you seek with the information you are providing online.

Remember as you are attempting to optimize your website, or when you have hired someone to optimize your website, that legitimate business practices always win out in the long run.

Also note that if you use very broad or general terms in the optimization of your website that you will not be targeting your actual buying audience and that you will simply be using "billboard tactics" to draw traffic to your site, rather than taking the time to find the people who actually want to purchase the goods or services you provide.

Don't be mislead into believing that you should be able to beat out companies who have been working on proving their relevance over the span of many years online in a very short time-frame.

You have to prove yourself online, just as you would have to prove yourself in any other aspect of the business world.

Getting attention, exposure and perhaps even calls is still not the only end that you need to meet either.

Once you get those calls, be sure to answer them with great service and reliable products so that you can not only turn your potential customers into long-term clients, but also so that you do not ruin your chances in business because of receiving a large number of negative client reviews who are often more than happy to let the rest of the world know that your business is the worst choice they could make.

SEO is many things. SEO is a beginning, a middle and a long-term maintenance project, but SEO is not an end.

You still have to close the sales and you still have to prove your worthiness through actions and dependability.

SEO also encompasses a wide variety of tasks and countless hours of work and upkeep. What you do today and sit on tomorrow may be surpassed by your competitor who is working on their SEO and online marketing strategy on a continuous basis.

Start SEO and keep moving forward!

When you do search for an SEO service, watch out for "guarantees" and promises of immediate results. You want lasting results if you are going to make your SEO efforts and expenses worthwhile for supporting your business maintenance and growth.

Thank you for reading SEO Standards for Beginners and please keep an eye out for more informative books on SEO by Alicia Crowder, owner of SEO Web Content Writing Solution.